BABSON'S BESTIARY

by Jane F. Babson ©1990
First copyright, unpublished, 1986

THE WINSTEAD PRESS LTD.
202 Slice Drive
Stamford, CT USA 06907

ISBN 0-940787-02-4

Library of Congress Catalog
Card No. 90-071155

Printed in Hong Kong by
Everbest Printing Company
Through Four Colour Imports, Ltd.
Louisville, KY 40205

Typeset by Goodway Printing & Graphics
Stamford, CT 06901

BABSON'S BESTIARY

by Jane F. Babson

THE WINSTEAD PRESS LTD.
202 Slice Drive, Stamford, CT USA 06907

This Book is Dedicated to
My Children,
David and Leila Jane

FOREWORD

The dictionary says that a bestiary was a medieval book in which animals were drawn and morals were told. In other words people were told how to behave. Artists drew pictures of animals they had seen and some of which they had only heard, believed in, or just imagined to be true.

You children of today have television as your bestiary, but we still have to know our world and what is in it. That is why I have drawn and written this book — for all of you who are learning to read.

Jane F. Babson

Is for Ape.
There are quite a few.
This one's not dumb —
He's looking at you.

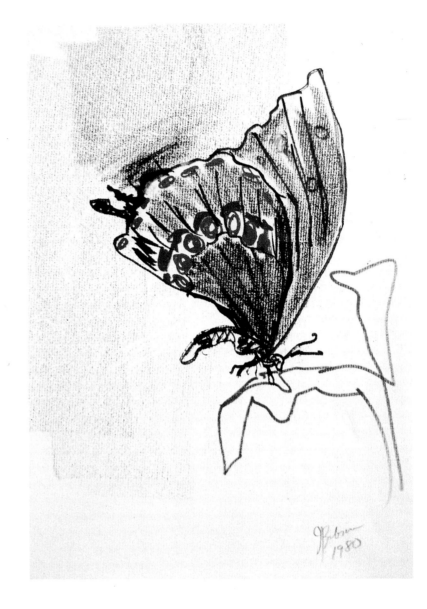

B

Is for Butterfly,
Which sails in blue air;
It flies — so can we —
But we must take care.

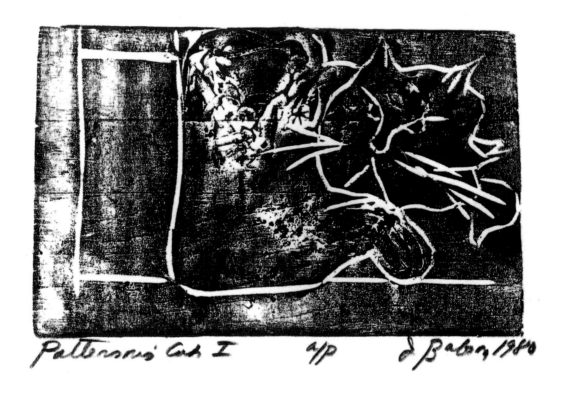

Patterson's Cat I   a/p   d Baban 1980

Is for Cat,
Not tame, but quite nice.
Leave him alone —
He's looking for mice.

D

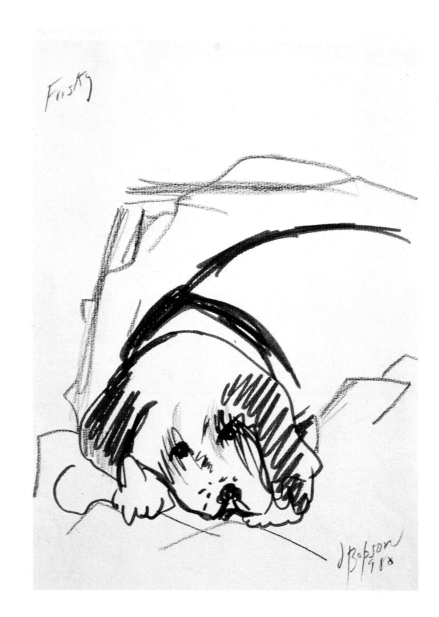

Is for Dog,
Man's friend and his pet.
This one's asleep,
Don't wake her just yet.

E

Is for Elephant.
Some *think* he may *think*.
If we don't do likewise,
He may be extinct.

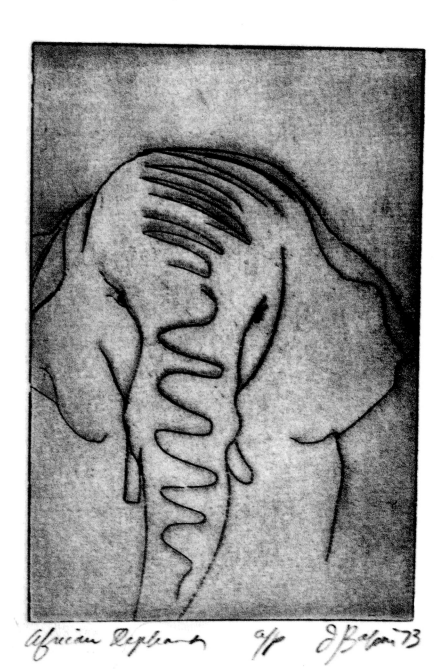

F Is for Fish,
Which swim in the sea.
These are pets, gold and black,
One for you, one for me.

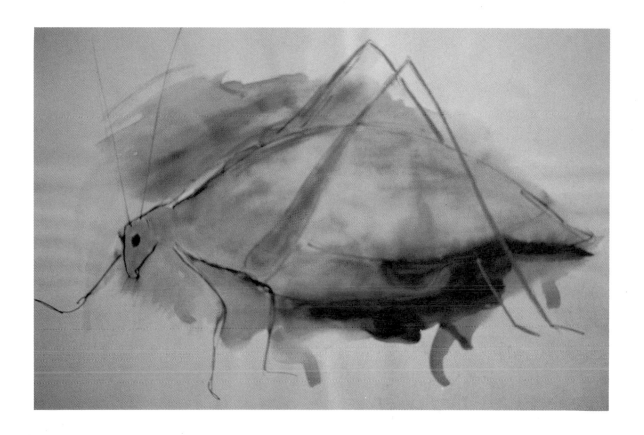

Is for Grasshopper.
He moves very fast.
When you see his green suit,
You know summer is past.

H

Is for Horse,
Here a sculpture quite great.
His stall's the British Museum,
Hey — that's not a bad fate.

I

Is for Iguana.*
A lizard so cold,
It's ancestor's the dinosaur,
Both vicious, I'm told.

*Pronounced e-*gwa*-nah

J

Is for Jaguar.
His family's the cat.
He looked forward and back
While in Mexico he sat.

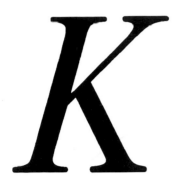**K**
Is for Kangaroo,
Christopher Robin's best friend.
If a zoo wants a live one,
To Australia it must send.

L

Is for Lion,
Beautiful, noble and wise.
Don't try to tease him,
Or you'll get a surprise.

M

Is for Monkeys.
Chatter, chatter and play.
Climbing a rope in the zoo,
While passing the day.

Monkeys 7/10 d.Palmer '80

N

Is for Nightingale.
Emperors kept her to sing;
With her voice quite fine,
She's a beautiful thing.

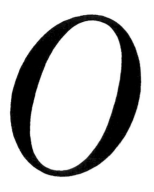

Is for Owl.
Do you think this one's cute?
She's really a bird
Whose call is a hoot.

Panda a/p L Babron 1980

P

Is for Panda.
Ling-Ling is her name.
She's a gift from China,
And on that rests her fame.

Is for Quetzalcóatl.*
From South America, a story —
Made of snake, bird and man,
With a character quite gory.

*Pronounced ket-sahl-*koh*-ahtl

R

Is for Rat,
It's presence a threat.
Perhaps it has a purpose,
But no one's found it yet.

S

Is for Squirrel
In a fur coat of grey.
Gathering nuts for the winter,
She's too busy to play.

T

Is for Turtle,
Old, boxy and slow.
Some live one hundred years,
For what — do you know?

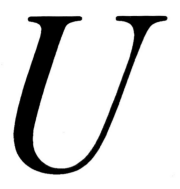

U

Is for Unicorn.
A horse with a horn?
Well, that's a big lie,
As sure as you're born.

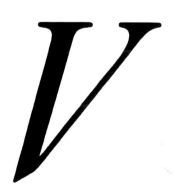

V

Is for Viper;

It's other name is snake.

This is a rattler quite deadly;

All care you must take.

Is for Walrus.
North Pole's ice is her palace.
She's flashing her whiskers,
Perhaps she's waiting for Alice?

X, Y

What is this?
Have I failed? Is it true?
Oh, no, not at all —
For X is a mystery,
And Y is for *You*.

Z

Is for Zebra.
Look, she's dressed up in stripes.
And this book now must end;
Why you've read it! Oh, cripes!

AUTHOR'S NOTE

This book is primarily illustrated by the graphic arts — my drawings, prints and photographs. Many of the animals in this book are represented by drawings, on-the-spot sketches with magic markers or pen studies. Letters C, M and P are woodcut prints, F is a serigraph, or silk screen print, and E and O are etchings. G, H and L are water colors; R is a Chinese ink brush painting. S is a collage (pasted paper and ink drawing). W is a mixed media (magic markers and water colors); J and Q are photographs.

With exception of A, N and O, which were done from stuffed animals, *viz.* the nightingale in The British Museum of Natural History, and U from my imagination, all the animals were drawn from life or sculpture in the United States and Great Britain. The photographs were taken in Mexico. Most of the prints and drawings in this book were made originally for children over the past twenty years.

THE END